Oceanic

Philip Wesley Comfort

2nd Enlarged Edition

Resource *Publications*

An imprint of *Wipf and Stock Publishers*
199 West 8th Avenue • Eugene OR 97401

Resource Publications
 An imprint of Wipf and Stock Publishers
199 West 8th Avenue, Suite 3
Eugene, Oregon 97401

Oceanic
Ocean-Inspired Poems
By Comfort, Philip W
Copyright©2004 by Comfort, Philip Wesley
ISBN 13: 978-1-59244-655-1
ISBN 10: 1-59244-655-8
Publication date 9/1/2007
Previously published by Feather Books, UK, 2004

INTRODUCTION

The poems in this volume were all, in some way or another, inspired by the sea or by the coastal lands near the sea. Life by the sea has its own rhythm and rhyme, verved by the winds and tide moving the waters. These poems, I hope, sway and roll with those rhythms. As you read them, do so out loud. Catch the oceanic spirit and drift away to the sea and beyond. Enjoy the good God Creator who still breathes into his creation the breath of life and wind.

The first section of poems are those inspired by living by the sea. The second section contains surfing poems. To me, as well as to other soul surfers, surfing is not so much a sport, as it is an adventure of one's soul journeying into the living spirit of the Creator. It is a way of getting close to creator God, the God who still moves, breathes, and manifests his being in ongoing, vivifying creation.

Take this book to the beach, let it get real sandy, and faded with sun. Read it out loud to the cadence of the waves. Or, if you can't get to the beach, let the poems take you there. Either way, enjoy.

Four of the poems in this volume appeared in another book of my poems, *Spirit Journey*, namely, "Iam," "surfer," "the beach is his," and "dogangel." Three poems in this volume were subsequently included in the anthology, *Pilgrimages*, edited by Walter Nash (in Feather Books): "earthrise sun," "couldn't make it out," and "dolphin dawn." The second edition of *Oceanic* includes 20 new poems (47-66), written from 2003-2007.

CONTENTS   page

Poems Inspired by the Sea

Surf Poems

1. oceanic

1.

windThrust windBend wingTurn sunRend skyChange
wavePush. peek. glacis. surge and suck. splash and swoosh.

ebb tide. fetch and flash. rise and fall. crest and crash.
wave break. sea splash. pound ground. kick. flush. push

'gainst my earth. rush gush tide flow shallowingDeep
clearingAir breakingBack whiteBurst in surge

froth downtow. the sea. the sea. lines of it.
tons of it. water creator dumping thumping

crashing crushing. long sea. open ocean. holding earth
through war and peace. long sovereign. lone lord.

untamed. uncut. untrammeled. undivided. moved me.
move me. make me oceanic. make me, sea.

2.

I step out of water and ocean falls off. I am mammal. land.
earth. defrocked and naked, I seek hermitage in recluse waves

and look long for overcast oceans to break fast
and take me. Down. Under. Away. Out. Back. In. To.

But here again I sit and contemplate my marlness
as I watch waves mount and mush, and wonder what's

our difference. As seafog sponges the coast like mist
over lovelost eyes, thinness between water and land fade.

I move, as it were, before the matrix Spirit hovering
somewhere between wet and wildness, hesitating to utter,

to blurt, "Let the land appear dry." Better it stay water.
the long surge of sea. the stretch over nothing but fetches.

water moving into waterness. dark hunkering under
darkness. no one there to call it hostile to the light.

nothing mammaling. swimming. sucking air. let not
the divide slice. better it be fog than forlorn. and rare.

3.
Its own creation, unscrolled and scrolling, a bodiless soul
taking shapes of waves, transfigured into cresting forms,

flashed into flesh it appears, then disappears in froth,
foam, blown into nothing by the spirits of zephyrs.

Sea and breeze, kindred ghosts, moisten imagination,
kick waves, wonder. Slip between thoughts and under –

they are miracleMaking. Nothing from them can be taken.
I am immersed again. Again I seek ablution, transfiguration.

To be rid of furtive flesh. To squirm from this body just once
and become the wave I surf, the wind I breathe. Free from mortal

me. A wave gone bodiless. Wind gone everywhere
into water–to crest, peel, crash, mush, splash, foam.

4.
I have not seen angel. Felt one, yes. Nor Jesus in flesh.
His Spirit roams earth, wet wanderer giving *living* water.

Until his face I see, I hear wild wetness of his word
stirring wind and waves. He sustains. Creating creation

as the sun swells yet again over our imagined horizon.
Never in the solidness of my flesh have I crossed

that line to find the plume thin into wind and sea.
But spirits come to me from yonder. Slim explorers

of the afterwave and now. They have seen more miracles
than fish. They penetrate the membrane between here and then.

Their spirit calls the ocean out of me. And I have returned
to sea. The voice so clear, as when I first heard the waves

breaking and God's presence as my own breathing.
I come, Lord, frontiering the ever of everlasting.

5.
    Nothing is more beautiful than the wave. coming from God
going back to spirit, it's manifest in so sleek a time and rhythm.

    leaving the horizon it swells it own shape and rhymes its line
as it moves serenely. music. magic. mystery of here and gone.

    a song of shape and unshaping. the deep smooth mound of
blue blooms, forms, curls, peels, plumes brighter than cloud, surges

    down the long line of sound, sagaciousness, and fury falling
into festive froth and riot of splurge surging fast and free.

    like bee diving into moving aqua pistil, drinking nectar,
I slide into you and out, higher than air, happier than suck.

nothing is more juicy than being in the wave. going with God, slipping into spirit. getting wet in so sleek a fall of rhyme.

6.

Waves wend me. send me places I haven't stepped. I haven't thought. oh, when the wave breaks its beauty open

like divinity undressed, God's unveiled as Spirit expressed, light is pushed out of darkness and moves euphotic.

Everywhere under over in and around, light breaks as waves snap and hurl their splendrous lumens into froth flame.

I Rise. Ride. Flare. Glide. Glow. Flow fantastic. An epiphanic flash of soul. Of ghost gone incarnate. Emaculate. Evanescent.

Unnamed. Unknown. Unchartered. Unfettered. Not boxed. Not coaxed. Not moved into a zoo. Not nailed upon a wall.

Not at all stopped, tamed, trammeled, flushed. The gush gladdens hope. The roar rages against all sages. Dive. Swim. Wash. Roll.

2. Kauai

unmanned ocean curls Kauai
      rides its lovers out to sea
and hurls them back again
      on roaring aqua surf
the raw sacred motion
      of savage holy union
primes procreation seen–
      sea gives birth to surf and sands
ocean erupts a naked island
      sprouting glistening palms
and waterfalls running
      to wet their wild nativity.
its mystic sway juices islanders
      with rains that come and go
from punched potent clouds
      covering Kilohana peak
where that voice still speaks
      and sings in Wailua's falls
flowing down Na Pali's cliffs
      rambling Waimea's trails.
I swear I've touched the words before
      but can't discern their sacred lore.

3. watersound

too much is made of meaning, too little is wrung from sound
rhyme is defunct uncool, rhythm untapped and snared
moderns can't hear rivers carving canyons
waves sanding shores
continents shifting in water
glaciers moving poles
(their sounding signifies nothing)
but it is not noise – no – when spheres sing to spheres
and deep calls to deep in language we can't fathom
the motion is not music
the music is not word
the word is not spoken
the speaker is not heard
it slithers mississippi and stares shiltehorn
it creeps sahara slowly under the utter sun

4. depths

a stripe upon a canyon wall
        where rivers forced a scar
the tracing is not just and square
as limned by some carpenter
it dips
        jags
                disappears
merges with other lines
then reappears
        in different form
it bears no record of what has lived
only what has been

no one examining the wear
will note the stroke of being cut
        all groans are garbled in untold rush
downward to the sea, then hushed
how
mute
the
deaths
that
forged
these
awful
depths

5. catch the meaning

I just missed the hissing bobcat bounding in the bush
and a siting of puma roused me
to search on the morrow he didn't reappear.
the marsh hummed as always with cicada strum
the stream sung as ever over fallen rock
if I were spirit everywhere I could watch.

other signs are fixed as sun moon stars
their constance carries the flight of day
and beaches boundaries for my swelling thoughts.
wave after wave connects the drifting continents
where natives spot the cheeta slinking past the dark
and fishers catch the meaning of a broken text.

Seabrook Island, South Carolina

6. this moment

bluefish running fast
the gulls chasing minnows tell
fishermen fling their poles in hope of catch
while translucent crosscurrent waves crash
in a wash of white and curl.
        as for me this moment
I'd rather still and hear
the sound between waves
the sense between thoughts
the distance between lovers
as a sunny day turns suddenly gray

Chattam, Cape Cod

7. whirling fury

sometimes
they can be tracked
mostly they move
their own mind
making the most
capable crazy
they don't plan attack
like reasonable men
but have a way
of taking over
when they siren
to shore
on the wheel
the round wheel
the wheel
within the wheels
the eye within
the round eye
circling unconsciously
furiously flashed
pushing the clock
backward to
heartpounding halt
as the engine
speeds by black
a sea-sucking
tongued funnel
whirling fury
on our land
through thin
structures
mostly man

July 11, 1996
Hurricane Bertha

8. Iam

known by the innocent Iam groped for soon enough
when lost to sense Iam chased, pursued
sometimes in a flash Iam seen in books
and caught in anguished looks
      I riverovermountainrocks
can't be snared or sepulchred
IamWavesFetchFrothFoamPelicanStorkGullLoon
Iam seaSpill reefBreak gullSplash rockCrash
tidePush moonPull fishFlush birdSwarm windDraft
      Iam succulentJuice MangoPapayaOrange
Iam undulatingAspen bucklingPine
waterOuzel slippingFall glacierShifting
movingMeadows sinkingFurrows
      Iam divinescent flowerooze sundrink
that brokenopen essence that flick that kick
that slightest touch of monarchlegs
on branchbend in floweryawn
      Iam caw crawl fishspurt grainsprout
bobcatBounding pumaSleekness forestRain
seapeeling earthbreaking sunsoaking lifescent
that earthturned wiff eyeglint joyburstAftersadness
sigh touch of invisibleQuick
      I Spiritmove intoEveryLivingThingIam
I dewdescend on spiders' webs
the diamond crystals in translucentSun
I chamelion green lizardbacks to brown
lighten murkiness Let darkness cloud
      I do not come to reason or defend
but transform U g LY to thin and flat to ROUND
ubiquitous, I cannot flee
                nor you me
IamFalconflightWindhold
Iam hermit crab's search for conch
man's dream other planets are not parched
Iam woundedmolluskpreciouspearl
Iam spiritBreathpneumaAir

IamRushFountainWingsMotion
no cistern can hold me square
		I MoveMentoMadness
console bereft in their despair sadness
by unexpected magnoliaBloom
the breaking of exoticScent
heaven's jar unscrewed and poured
		whatever has being has being in me
IamMeaning IamTruth IamYou–
can't you see me in a thousand figures
lovely limbs, uncommon faces
signatured, distinct, unscrolled
each takes its shape from within
and shouts to the glories, IAm
		I will never be endangered though hunted
by all religions who haven't figured
Iam tideSurge windDrop treeFall
mushroomSprout spriggedLeaf treeRot
s t r e a k e d sunset blackcatdarkness
Iam tidechange sucked back over smooth stones
clacking in liquid s w o o s h and waveSurge
		can't you see Iam zoe?
all that ISaliveISalive with me
the peaTendril reaching for staked post
the redFox chasing bald pink sun
the mother milking twins with double tits
I feed all – Iam nutrient never spent
I sustain flesh with spirit – they are lent
until I take them back again.
this is not cruel or fluke or fair
this is what is and what is meant
		this galaxy has not spun forever
but I have always been
nothing could expand to be as Iam
and nothing can diminish me
as the tall grass waves in the wind
don't think it has no thought for me --
freshly mown, smell its sweetSacrifice

18

so are each of the trillion deaths to me
the squishedAnts scream and hooked fish
(their end is no less human)
        I cannotstop or backlook on what I was
for Iam vineblood humanserum spit and sperm
sap of Marchmaples Rainsoaked sweetcane
chickorycluster poking blue
through speckledgray rockcrack
Iam mountainlava oceancurrent
d o l p h i n g l i d e a n d p l u n g e
seahawk s w o o p ClawandTongue
fishwriggle flash and fetch
        Iam unboxed light exploding atoms
catch a glimpse of the topquarx smashing
but Iam thinner than can be scanned
the space surrounding atoms Iam
and the place that atoms are
        I can crawl into a sandcrab's hole
or blackholes cram with denser light
I can permeate the crooks of mind
coloring them with evil or with right
though I weigh nothing
I sit heavy on the guilty
and refuse to forsake those who curse me
Iam as faithful to spirit as spirit is to me
        don't think Iam evolution
I journey my biography
for Iam as Iwas and willbe as Iam
I cannot be ForestedFetteredForgotten
Iam aftermilennia afterHaveComeandGone
and the earth has no morsels left to give
Iam amillion mouths at once
underOnAbove the scalloped masses
a sea of leaves revealing this:
the floweringWheat is sure as my lips
for Iam always and always is

9. visit to the sea

suffering fast food, tollways, cramped legs
he drove to the coast to catch some wind
                    to comb the beach for conch
which bagged back to the city compensate the ear
here and there
                    he meandered shallow shoals
admiring tide carvings and sloping rippled canyons
stepping into pools of darting minnows
                    and rays trapped thin as sunlight.
looking off aways he spotted dolphin
                              humping the horizon
and pelicans penetrating glass
                    invisible, like music, the wind picked up
and played the sea as if it were harp
each wave falling in rhythm to the hum
          he stripped to the waist and plunged
sea-soaked, salt-rinsed, head-drenched in tumbling rollers
slammed into sand, a smattered shell not going back.

10. La Jolla beach

the missionary first to La Jolla's coast
must have pilgrimed through Torrey-pined mesas
up chapparel covered canyons to seacliffs' edge
and–ah!–a crescent sweep of zoatic ocean
set atulku-like between stretched limbs of land
cragged cliffs, cavernous promenades
and bald brown island rocks standing in surging surf
populated here and there by colonies of sunning pelicans
and multicolored seals stuffed with halfinger and kelp
near an encampment of Kumiyay dancing under mooncast
around a keruk facing dead east
mourning and chanting, "katoumi goes to your house"

would these who chased the Great Spirit
with goathide drums and mushroom trances
make host for Jesus' living ghost?

the winds kicking from the west snatched smoked ash
of a dear deceased and carried his second soul
beyond brown canyons' yawn and black bears

morning moved the missionary
toward seasound and seasmell
a swell of kelp, sunlight, seals, and greens
were tossed toward the littoral
as a freshly poured libation–
he smelled sea, breathed sea, deep sea
uprooted, experienced, and pungent
(his nostrils told him quicker than tongue)
the scent, stronger than sacrificial smoke,
intoxicates the most sober men
and stirs them to acts of madness

kerukless this unmourned martyr
as bald and crazy as island rock
was left to the shining surging sea

11. ripped

the ocean is salty this morning

      so are my tears

mercurial, silvergray, expensive ink
spilled across a parchment page
before the damp sun broke

      so does my heart

Africanorange and Africanwinds shimmer the sea

      we shared exotic dreams

the waves peel down the line
pumped by a distant hurricane

      your leaving rips me

I paddle out and take another peeling right
and then another, and still another
until my shoulders ache, legs cramp

      and I am crushed

again I paddle out
and wait with others for another set
driven by Caribbean wind

      not knowing what I'm thinking

as we watch half a rainbow arch
climb to heaven but not bend down

half our hopes are broken

as the sea begins to calm
and turns inkblue, running
soft across the parchment page

primed and presaged

August 28, 1999
the day my son Jeremy moved from Pawleys Island

12. wave

inscrutable abysmal
  your genesis is darkness
    lost in shapelessness, void
      an obscure voice speaks you
        pushes you to pilgrimage
          there is no will to stop
            as you undulate cap froth
            and you are hurricane driven
          by storms by fetch by sound
        passed vessels safe and sunk
      you are the Maker in motion
    the globe's visible undulation
    the breathing of the sea
  our planet's potency and pull

we are drawn to the coasts
  to watch your glory mount
    from some invisible thrust.
      with perfect curve and verve
        you then bowbend and kneedrop
          with brightness tumbling overhead
          as you flop in your conking roar
          (your own applause and praise)
        as another martyr dropping behind
      is just as quickly glorified and razed.
    so pacific are these separate deaths
    these revelations of soul
  that we gather by seabreak
and pray this is how we go

13. ocean sun

1.
lull and lunge. lunge and lull. water falling upon water.
      no shore to take the fall. liquid cymbal dropped
on liquid cymbal in the dark sound of it all. rush and roll.

      roll and rush. but not on shoals, sandbars, reefs.
deep from caverns the waves leaped lunged plunged spilled.
      falling from dark pitch. crash. crush. roar. sizzle.

requiem's breaking dirge. the surge. the slosh.
      the rush crush crash between each fetch and flush
in long stretches of nothing but darkness pushing water

      into blacker spaces. faceless. mirrorless. unconscious
water making itself seas, waking itself to its own existence
      in list and yaw. in plunge to deep in depths of gone

going deeper a strangle of water suffocating earth. a liquid ring
      as round as nimbus moon–but no glow, only gloom
in the dirge of surge upon surge flapping fishless fetches

      lonely stretches of horizonless seas seizing seas.
a tumble of black rolling into black and back again into nothing
      but wash wave lunge surge lull crash flush churn.

this sea a monster heaving, heeling in heavy wetness,
      in dark so fat nothing could wriggle between the cracks
lay leviathan lay crocodile on all paws, fanning its serpentine

      tail over what used to be fecund delta, lumined soil.
allwasWaterwithoutlight allwasDeepwithoutlife, a desert of sea
      everywhereGoingnowhere, for there was no horizon.

no separation of sea from sight. no beach. no wind of light
      to open/ break/ bleak bands/ cut/ slash/ fish darkness out
until Spirit spoke and smacked damp black in half

2.

an eyelid cracked the dawn. the sultry shroud lifted
      and the single eye unveiled sky, beamed seas
as the lit disk emberorange surged hot from burning styx.

      exorcised murkiness, swallowed shadows between waves,
made cool waters rise and spirit from the earth.
      it was a day for wind taking light and throwing it

all around between the shades and troughs. for drawing
      the long thin horizon line, as circular as the eye
who made it. it was a day for epiphany of color, for the parousia

of the sun's soft skull rupturing the oval horizon
      flushing it bloodshed red, raw and strange
more crimson than color (hyacinth's firstborn blazing bloom)

      wiping blackness out of night. stripping sea
of its mythic mystery. slaying leviathan of its lair and lore
      until evening came rare with spiritwinds

swiping 'cross horizon's stretch a murderous birth:
      crimson brim, mallow crescent, ironhot ladel
tipped over, spilling molten light in lava stream

      on lapping lapis lazulum turning green to blue
black to moon. and then again–after sucking some sleep from
      night's rind, the sun poked the circle of grim darkness

climbing in recurring blooms up gladiola's stem
      popping one after one in cloned effulgence
till bending the branch with glory's weight

      the topmost lobe began to make its arch
above the beloved blue ocean, brother to the silent sky
      mothermouth of every birth and every thirst

3.
the mounting. cresting. pearling. flip. flap. fall. roar.
        the liquid rush. swoosh. sizzle. instant art
splashed. splurged. fanned out. crested. scalloped.

        an ocean tongue lapping earth–the shore is ocean lips,
the waves its mouth–lulling, moaning, spuing foam
        from fall fetch pitch crash crush comes

seagull's call and cry. mackerel's flash. dolphin's push and play
        in saltsprayed sunlight. moonlit turtles stroking beaches.
waterserpents slithering. angelfish dancing. whales moaning.

        but there was not a man to scan the ocean sun
in hue shift more subtle than skyshift afterstormblack,
        bottomblack, sharkblack with yellowfoam turning brown

greenbrown in swarms of waves one after another breaking
        in bluefroth into so many greens, hundreds of them
more than the forest trees and plants, a roving jungle

        of verdant greens holding sunrays. lit greens in translucent
beams. springgreens popping with visible fish. summercool
        bluegreens. layered greens in euphotic shadows

but there was not a soul to catch the color switch from murkiness
        to virescence, the mellowing of duskgreen from emerald
to reseda, and all the in-betweens, the hazel, jade, and aquamarine

4.
        sea and water. sun and water. moon and water.
as mist rising from the earth. they came rising from
        the ground and wet spirit, staring at the sun, moon,

water–oceans of it. they walked under the skies–oceans of it,
        stars in it, white waves of it. and then there were clouds
between them. better for sunrise. sweeter for sunset. for gazing

27

for wondering, for listening to waves make beaches,
to rain make rivers, to Spirit wandering in the wind. between
waves and thoughts, they walked the shore marveling

they were and were not kingfish, seagull, dolphin, dusk or dawn
wondering why they had come at all, figuring the wave
rush, crush, splash, lunge had pushed them from sea to shore.

they desired migration in the glistening waves
in the going somewhere with the sun beyond darkening horizons,
for they were island and all their dreams a sea.

5.
as the sun rounded again and rolled across the scabbed sky
a winged scarab once dunged with darkness
rising plump with festal promise over virgin waves and wind

the blossoming of a rooting sea. they made this disk
a signet ring and pressed it to their fluid thoughts
stoneround and hard as memory – inside this cartouche

they etched their hopes as it Kephri rolled into the seas again
and lost its way in water–molten as Re and lost as life.
they prayed it would spread its wings across the thin horizon

as it was killed slowly on the sea's backside–a brown
goingdown sun turning tideflow to rasberry, violet, mauve
as if dye from a cerculean mollusk had been squished

smearing skies phoenecian, purpling the plunging surf,
painting egrets magenta and the eyes of fishermen red
who gazed passed the phoenix beaches to the ocean's tug

6.
        while the sunbird rose, flinging its gray dark ashes.
the bent benu straightened, flaring wings into heaven's clouds,
        filling sailors with farflung reveries of exotic banks.

but a bulging thunderhead bullied their morning, bent headdown
        hunchbacked over the slim sea sucking up seaswirls
with multiple tongues. waterspout after waterspout pillared

        their horizon as the colosus looking more minotaur
than bull soaked in gray smothering the light was wet
        with warring, was white when done and passed off

as Proteus shepherding flocks of porpoise away from the sun.
        cold creatures crowded deep waters standing 'round coals
of blazed fire. the flushing sun oranged their gray beards

        pinked their blustering massive heads, turning their bodies
and swords bloodred as they cruised the vista looking for land.
        the beacheads feared them rising from the sea, mounting

in long straight lines with stiff solidarity following Neptune's
        dolphindrawn chariotconch, desperately wanting
to desperately matter, making charge to their turf

        mightily bursting on their forted shores, splattering into a
billion whiteheaded ghosts, all screaming they made it earth
        as they weakened in their own drowning waters

7.
the anatole arose, revealing to fishermen in light weightier
     than the sea, with words quicker than fishflashing
the glory of everlastingwater freshfetched from forever

     and washed in seven oceans before it rivered all earth–
it was broken. lightbroken. suntaken in the waterspout
     and flashflood of pierce and plunge. dark torrents of the

abyss were swallowed than hallowed into water, into light.
     the sun slid up the smooth palm of dawn, a rusty gold
coin pushed out from closed fist by some invisible thumb

     and flipped. it made slow arched ascent over the gleaming
global ocean until it dropped again in another hand
     bloodied and cleansed for having been spent.

we thought it was God who turned the earth overnight
     without spilling any stars and just slightly sloshing some
water, through which the sun dolphined and dawned

     flashing out a fiery corridor from sea's end through
runnels to our soaked feet, inviting us to walk that aisle
     but knowing our limits we headed north to the pier–

each step followed like moonbeam. we were marked.
     commanded to take notice: three dogs barked, kicking up
grains. sandpipers scurried in and out of shallow pools

     crabs took to their holes, pelicans bobbed, seagulls dove,
kingfish desperately tried to change fins to wings,
     while we stood still and made the worship human

14. gnarled

skyward
a gnarled bonsai twisting
                on rockfaced   seacliff
worn slick by perpetual wash of waves
bent backward
        by aging wind
twisted
        and
 turned
        for having followed
                the seasons of the sun

only the sea eagle has lighted
        on its
        contorted
torso
        people passing in boats have gawked
        wondering how it ever grew

some deep sap
must sustain it
some hidden sea
pump life into its veins
for there's usually
    some green leaves
                and sometimes in spring
                    a flower or two

15. wave watching

the unsettled breezes master you
        west wind: stiff small waves. spray.
east: choppy mushy sections closing quickly
        northeast: firm rugged potent cliffs
southwest: with a swell, prime and heady.
        by wind and sun your color shifts
more subtle than skyshift
        afterstormblack, bottomblack, sharkblack
with yellowfoam turning brown
        greenbrown in armies of waves
one after another breaking in bluefroth
        into so many greens, hundreds of them
more than forest trees and plants
        at least, to me, who lives ocean
you are my roving jungle–
        verdant greens holding sunrays
lit greens in widelight beams
        springgreens popping with visible fish
summercool bluegreens inviting surf
        layered greens in euphotic shadows
the color switch of soundswish
        from murkiness to virescence
the mellowing of duskgreen
        from emerald to reseda
and all the bluegreen inbetweens
        hazel, jade, aquamarine
but nothing is more potent than silver
        quicksilver running down the waves
sleekgray in rainfall pitch and pull
        each drop making its moment
smoothing out wavemounds
        a desert of water mounting and falling
all else is graylost

the clouds, the sea, the sky, and surf
all is melting unmoulded silver
never to be trophy cast

Pawleys Island

16. they pilgrim what we ponder

fluted sounds breathed out
into distant seagreen hollers–
the souls we thought we knew pass
while the tune we tapped lingers

unladened unmaned ships sent out
into wild darkgreen rollers–
the spirits we tried to tame go
while the course we hold wanders

smoke rising from snuffed candles
into the swirled blueblack yonder–
the saints we knew we loved left
while they pilgrim what we ponder

17. I pray you anyway

I know you're not God. no answers.
but I pray you anyway. and hope
you hear me naming you above
these southern pines and stars
swaying and shifting as ocean waves.
a thousand times in my mind
(successive unsurfed breaks
plunging into froth and sand)
you're here and then you're not
(flattening thinly back to sea
returning in the splurging flash)
I've imagined you to come
from where together we had been
but you moved on to mountains

18. still the sun

a southern balm washed its way into our air
a soltice swash wiping out winter
calling back monarchs, memories, and waves
recapturing Eden from the frozen grip of cherubim
         if Joshua could still the sun
tumbling ash freeze Herculaneum
and glaciers petrify sappy pines,
I'd ask God to immortalize this hour
         but etherized butterflies escape glass
and mounted seatrophies snap back
for there's no keeping what can't be kept–
redemption will come, not regret

19. long strong

the strong cloud
takes the man out of mind

drastic lightning spooks darkness
heavy surge cannot be tamed

but nothing is fiercer
than the long strong kiss

can it withstand?

roots spread deeper into hard clay
searching running water

palms bending the wind
color heaven

while the long sun
takes distance out of time

20. So far, not good

So far, not good.
Her mind has taken her better places than she has been.
The sea is no solace;
it keeps leaving her and spreading into strange spaces.

"You have hollowed out my being and asked me to sing.
I will not. And cannot.
I have traveled too far for anything but melancholy."

The old beachwalker carries way too many burdens,
heavier than the sea.
But only the sea, the deep sea can drown them.
It has thrown its corpses on the sand.
She collects them, smiles, and imagines she was young.

I have seen her become thinner than the flat beach
slimmer than her shadow at dusk
skinnier than the horizon she pictures, as she tries
to erase the long bumpy line and scratch a better ending.

She will dissolve into this air, this streak of sun
and live on something other than water
but not on words–so thin so insubstantial so unable.

The long straight answer of things is not that anymore–
at least in what she's become.
She needs angels quick, spirit touch, God's soul
and flesh, because so far it's not been good.

21. moon, wind, worm

rising fullbodied in the east
        triumphing earth, dragging ocean
in its wake, pulling heavy tidewaters
        to build, brim, break, crest
sanddunes and pillared homes
        throws piles of water everywhere
flocks of it, swarms, seagulling,
        hovering, settling, squatting–
effulgent nightdominant moon

westwaking, raking pines
        bristling elms, arching aspens
in the treetrunktall sky
        it whirs between coves
resurrects waves, ghosts fetches
        presences God in eardrop silence
falls festooned, spirit rises,
        numbs bones, cools downcast faces –
allpotent earthdominant wind

northborn transformed
        chrysallis makes solo farflight
living on God, on angels,
        on wings as thin as wind
with thinner mind it pilgrims
        above myriad meadows
mountains seacoasts and men
        to its panagyrous heaven
in festive flocks of orange –
        transcendent monarchal worm

fall 2002

22. wind spirit

wind spirit, you move sea. walk waves. plunge hurlers into flesh,
flash, peel, crush, crash. they spirit away like so many other holy
ghosts I've rode. you phantom water, incarnate curls and bends.

you open sun and close like purple rose at dark. you lift stars.
you drift, shapeshifter, sea-lifter. you drip, drenched. cool.

I've caught your face. unveiled. lifted. smooth. serene, when
and only when you show yourself then speed away. still,

wind spirit, you return unpredicted. unwritten. apocalyptic.
seizing the skies, you make earthrise. sunbend. cloudfall.

waterless hands await you. cupped. dry mouths open. unearthed
mourners looking for souls. you come to drums. by dances.
through flutes. in songs. you are muse and music. blend

poet and oracle. shape and shifter. shade and light, wavetop
bender. the slender inbetween. take flight, sender of dreams,
make light the monarchs' wings and go, going away. good God,

wind spirit, what have you brought? long memories of oceans.
of sailors. of lovers lost. the deep couldn't hold you back?

moans must you carry? cross? siezed moments. the last drops.
I've lost your voice, wind spirit, in louder pains of flesh. attack.

pierce. I'm hollow. your lute. sing. the prophet bends. send word.
gust. make me spirit too. make me flesh of you. open. crack

the dawn. pump everliving breath. breathe in me and I am soul.
let go and I am sand. dust. earth. dry. dead. forsaken. limp.
a lump. O, fuse. force. be fierce. my firmament fill. flash. flood.

wind spirit, I am gashed. poured. watered. wet. winded. liquid.
melted. you undressed me. made me holy. ghost ungone.
I am spirit. unborn. undead. flow. muse and music. beyond

and in. over and through. there is not end. beginning. just you,
wind spirit, lifebreath, quickening verve, sustaining wings,

limbs, and lips. guts and gall. voice, call, coo, and crow. carrion
is not you. nor anylivingthing. light of eyes. sap of flower. sing

and song. move and movement. wind spirit, I am longing to be
rent and sent. given and gone. coming and going. flung and fling.

slimmer. quicker than God gone to ghost and wind gone to wave,
wind spirit, you slip between the earth and silence. over barriers
of sound. you are round. always round. never gone, good giver.

23. dogAngel and dolphins

living on water and air and my love
I thought you'd make it to the warm days –
how you craved the sun as your body thinned
you still flared your nostrils to the wind
but couldn't chase. there was no more prance
left in you, though you wanted to please.

the last good day together we shared the beach
and winter sun with two families of dolphins
no more than a paddle away. they lit the ocean,
leaped, flipped, danced, dallied, pranced, played.
I know, Charlie, I know how you wanted to join –
you waded the frigid surf but couldn't swim.

the last grim days dragged slow as old January
and I spoke nothing significant and couldn't change
the end, as we watched one cold sunset after another
die. and I clung to keep the spirit of us alive
but I couldn't keep you from going to ghost –
I read it in your desperately sweet brown eyes.

the moment you left I went weeping to the drenched sea.
I passed some children throwing bread and laughing
as a swarm of cawing seagulls circled overhead.
then they shouted with delight into the cold mist:
"look, dolphins!" and I saw the twins streaming silver,
sea's angels, as sure of where they headed as eternity

January 31, 2003
the day a glorious soul of a golden retriever named Charlie
left this earth and went to the next

41

24. surfer

the sea is glass, a pond to skate on
a mirror for the sky's changing faces.
young tanned men come and go to shore
with strapped boards and fixed memories
but tide after watched tide drops their mood
like the half-lit moon in the west
but so does the pressure
       the ground slowly swells beneath the sea
bumping up substantial successive ridges
a southwestern holds them firm and strong
as they move along, rising higher and thicker
until they peak and trim a hundred yards long
each wave peeling off, dropping, pearling
as if some invisible finger slid down an ivory keyboard
       but the sound is not piano–it's percussion:
tight snare roll, zildjian crash, morocco sizzle
as the surf breaks and stallions toward shore
past darting mullet and skimpering sandpipers
to the ankles of these bronzed islanders
bound to the sea and the board that takes them
beyond the chop, breakers, and roll
       where they watch the culmination
of arduous African migration
storm-swelled over far fetches
wall after liquid wall moves toward shore
as the surfers take off in fierce anticipation
of the thrill of standing under that curl
that can thrust or crush the interloper
who dares to call himself surfer

July 7, 1997
Pawleys Island, South Carolina
for Peter

42

25. first rides

a dreamed-of morning
for riding slowforming rollers near the pier
for taking sleek quick runs
                    and soft salt falls
for diving into waves
                    as if I were seagull

my only companions–looping dolphins and languid sun–
didn't scan how board/feet/wave/run
but it doesn't matter for they know no wave ever lasts

and I don't mind it passing
          like the last best set
for another is bound to form on my horizon

The Isle of Palm's Pier
South Carolina

43

26. Twilight at Cape Hatteras

first faint above thin pink wisps
the moon ascending heavy surf now faces
straight across a spit of swaying seaoats
the sun burying itself into earth
and bloodying the western scape.
the crescent star has the glory of its fallen twin
and lights the last two surfers taking turns
mounting and descending windwhipped peaks
until they tire and retreat to sand
where nocturnal glow claims dominion
as it rises higher on seasaw's end
tilting upward on seagull's wing.

August 16, 1997

27. a long right

a long right
a steep right
a hollow right
a memorable right
never interrupted by fall
a long right
a good right
a smooth right
an eternal right
that is what I look for
in the crooked
most of the time
I can't find it
but once in a while it's there
peaceful like uncalculated air
rising on my hemispheres
waiting for me to catch it
hanging there to fetch it
and when I get it, it gets me
there is nothing as good
nothing as free
not anyone has hallowed out
such a sacred groove
as one who is creative God

April 1998
Pawleys Island, South Carolina

45

28. La Jolla Shores

these waves have come from where I've never been
I know them only in their end
these bending tumblers, sleek divers, plunging headers
who spirit the *skene* one majestic minute
then just as quickly ghost away.
what puissance primed, pumped, and pushed them
into performance is never told by their faces
which we glide across leaving impermanent traces
of having caught them in their glory

La Jolla Shores near Scripps
San Diego, California
June 9, 1998

46

29. fun waves

jumps flash dash tropical dark
              quick thick glory breaking
dolphins splurge spin
                  dive splash
pelicans
fall
from
sky
like
rain
while southwest spirit lifts waves
sustains
a surfer
      slicing sideways
              down steepsleek wall
of white chasinghimlikesnowslide
weaves in and out
         of furious surf
mounts up–brute stallion–takes off
cuts spins swirls
        landing in trough
              of sweet smooth sunned froth

summer 1998
Pawleys Island, South Carolina

30. dawn surf

sunless
sea and sky melt into each other's lines
      like quicksilver, mercurial, sleeksmooth
in glistening grays slipping cool over the horizon
      a comfortable dark, serene and unoppressive
over the wingspreadglide of egrets
      and rolled waves bumping up like dolphinbacks
in the unscrolled moist oceanmorning mist
      settles in like pelican flock
hovering landing floating bobbing biding
      in the graywash, capecodish wetness
argent at surf's break, otherwise as solemn
      and silent as the surfers' wake

November 18, 1998
Pawleys Island Pier, South Carolina

48

31. intruder

the ocean gray in the morning
usually catches some leftover light
from the moon
and there's always breaking
here and there some white churn which I slide down at eyes' height
beneath my feet
jacks dart blues dodge kings plunge
as I their surf intrude
paddling back I spot a mullet host
a gray ghost hovering on the green
popping jumping sliding whirling
the corraled won't leave their kind
fearing together is better
than escaping on their own.
slowly as the sun gallows in the hung mist
the commune is martyred
by invisible insidiousness – the jaws of ancient law
while I lay thin on my board
pretending to be invincible, watching the shade drift
now slimmer
than the horizon

July 1999
Pawleys Island, north of the pier

32.   taste of wind

fishless and thick with sea
dark waves storm-wintered
stroke the shore with blackness
and push every soul away
except a few blackgarbed surfers
and one old man pushing a nor'easter

when the moon is long and sun thin
we forget the smell of sun and taste of wind

this flaw ends as suddenly as the seahawk snatch
as quickly as the next bareback catch of wave
glistening with glory in the curl and froth –
these whiteheaded waves are the breaking of age
good for the young to ride and shout
pleasant for the old to watch and contemplate

when the sun is long and moon thin
we remember the smell of darkness and taste of wind

April 21, 2000
for Peter on his 18th birthday

33. storm surfing

silversea turns mauve in greydawn
    flat as horizon flat as sky
        as I lay thin on my board and wait.
I cannot see but know the sun
    behind a veil of cloudsmear
        there is halfyellow in the air
        darkyellow in the waves
    as they curl peel drop disappear
    into ocean unscrolled across this stretch of earth
unsaying while waiting for some significance
undisturbed except for plump pelicans diving thin
    and dolphins rocketing the surface
    exposed black to sun and rare to earth
        splashing flat and loud and down and gone
    into the deepgreen goinggray undertowed
as suddenthunderheads press the surface
    pushing a wilderness of waves my way
ghosting darkhooded bentover and brave
    through a million spears plunging individually
into water (more water than thirsty God)
    all is wet all is water all is soaked
the sky the sea the air and me –
    then just as suddenly the skies depart
and I spot a wave swelling
    bluebodied bareheaded resurrected
from its grave of flattened gray.
    I know that I must take it on
        or it will take me down.

July 28, 2000
Pawleys Island, South Carolina
the south groin

34. no separate gull of ocean

the ocean sound is round. no separate gull of ocean.
    no wave of its own unfolding. up and down the coast
they'd been invoking an epiphany of wind on sea.

    how stoked after a long drought of catching next to nothing
to see it come – pumped, curved, conched, stretched out,
    peeling under dark clouds heavy air surging from the south –

a gaggle of waves, whitetopped, lining up, and pearling.
    paddling till our arms ached, backs tightened, legs cramped
eyes squinting in sunbursts through colorshapes running

    thickly, ghosting water, making all the white to grave rise.
froth, hoot, holler. Waves! who knows of tomorrow—
    they may thin in west winds. they may calm halcyon at dusk.

but this day is goodGodcreated and we are graced to take these breaks.
    the paddle. push. the jump. thrust. the weave. cut. the curve. slice.
the ride. glide–down long glacis, silent before crush, thick and sweet

    as the boardturn swish, I and wave. wave and I in one rush
of naturalness. of no telling of the sea from me, as I charge its break
    and wake and am thrust into sudden sacred hollowness

and come out flushed. flashed. having grasped the surge of, the pulse of
    the primal ocean winging wet wild flinging soaked piles
of mounting moving waters making breaking taking me along and down.

March 2002

35. Playa Guiones

Nosara, with mountaincrested beaches
    and offshore breezes on swelling sea
azure, clear, and primed, a soulsurfer's dream
    (can't believe it!) that you gave me
longstrong rides on pristine waves–
    (how sweet!) the shape, the peak, the feel
of dropping in before the peeling break
    of sliding along a headhigh crest,
a mounting moving liquid face,
    of tucking under the windwhipped curl
as it began to bend (and thought would fall),
    but the wall held stiff by offshore gust
as I thrust into its hallowedness
    and entered a blessed sphere
where there's nothing but wind-and-sea,
    and I, an awed intruder (o spirit!),
who then slid out into foaming froth
    where a rainbow spray appeared
as miraculous as the wave (I caught it!)

January 5, 2001
Playa Guiones
Nosara, Costa Rica

53

36. the beach is his

the beach is his. he makes it. the darting minnows
         in surge, suck, sally. the sandpipers scurrying
         between swooshes. the dallies with clawing crabs.
the pelicans bobbing on the sea like sun.
the swim, the search in crushed waves for the stick I pitched.
the fetch, prance, strut – like a majorette, he waves the stick
         as high in the air as he can get it.
               he is good so good. it is his universe.
those who stroll by sense, catch, smile, and share the glow
         as we kick our way through the shallows
northwardheaded – I with board in hand and he with stick in jaw –
         and slosh our way to the northern spit
where I begin to surf nor'eastern shifts and slide winddown
         southbound breaking lefts, all the while trailed
by my companion who watches my catches and follows my drift –
excited by every ride, he runs along, my terrestial shadow.
and even if I mingle with a swarm of other blackgarbed surfers
         he stays fixed on me until I ride the last wave to shore
where I am met in the shallows by the sweetest soul
         with dance, swagger, primal joy, contagious happiness.
he wants more. so much more. never to leave the surging sea—
to chase dogs, rays, and falcons, to fetch, catch anything called life
         but I exhausted soaked and spent, coax him toward the exit,
where we pass many a local who don't known my name
nor I theirs, but they call out anyway: "Hey, Charlie! how's the surf?"

October 2002
for Charlie, golden retriever

37. surfing the storm

along the jagged horizon as in a Serengeti migration
    the wind shoves a herd of waves hurrying ahead of storm
gusting a gaggle of waves, a swarm of surf in torrid downpour
    deserting the sea to a watery wilderness pitching cresting falling.
the only white in all this world is wavecrash foam and froth
    the clouds, sea, sky, surf smear. mingle in a world awash.
wind is rain and rain wind. no sun to tell the time. only the tide.
    in all this drenched gray the only lumen is surfbreak and wit
while we ride the heave break snap curl of the hurling seabend
    juiced with cloudbursts and surfers clinging on, flinging on
the pumped lunging sea flung and flattened, flung and flattened
    in seabend break and snap. wet with hunger, cold, and wild
waves, we don't surrender till much too much beach appears.

September 2002

55

38. surfing Hawaii

What do you say – eyes full of tears, lump in throat –
to your youngest son, standing half a foot taller than you,
about to go off for a half year to Hawaii to surf the big ones?
"You are taking my whole heart with you. I am crushed.
Don't you. Not Waimea, please. In winter. The North Shore."
But I just pray: "O Lord, the sea is yours. You made it.
My son is yours. You made him. Keep them both alive."

The stars are cold tonight. Frozen. Unmoved. But as the sea never
ceases, I cannot ever stop being your father. Anxious. Excited.
Glad for your journey. Sad for our parting. It's death – each exodus.
Until then, take your dreams and stuff them with as much reality
as you can. Cram your days with as many waves as your body can
handle and your eyes can see. Eat, drink God in epiphanic sweetness,
for the earth is the Lord's in all its full and crazy exoticness.

November 2002
for Peter

39. Nosara: a journal

Escaping December dumping cold on the Carolinas
we flew from icebound Charlotte to tropical Liberia
and got a taxi with a Tico on whom we spilled
our mal Espanol – lots of laughs and shouts –
"no problema" as we drove through muddy streams
and bumpy roads from Nicoya to Nosara, Costa Rica,
passing each poquita villa with unmowed football fields
netless goalposts and open air festival halls–
until we arrived at Nosara–ah, Nosara! pristine
junglemountain leaping from ocean yaw and breathing sea
spiriting through cotamundi, armadillos, howling monkeys,
azure mariposa and indigo magpie riding zepherous gusts
bending bamboo, teaks, bananna, sleek palms
blending with rhythmic pulse of percussing waves
shorepounding through sunsoaked days and moonglow nights.
Ah, Nosara you bring good memories like a returning swell:
la bonita mar, las olas poderosas, los monos en los arboles,
las mariposas azure, los Ticos con los sonrinas suellas.
There we gazed at the Pacific glimmering under la luna media
revealing las oleajas pure and potent, pumping on playas Guiones.

session uno, Domingo manana
Coming from the Atlantic where waves bunch up like cloth,
I was thrilled to see the long spaces between each wave
as it built, peeled down the line–the aqua blue chased
by white churning froth, wave after wave, peeling to the right
and to the left, with sets coming in a foot overhead.
I had Guiones to myself and the sun brimming over the mount.
I paddled out, heart pounding, taking a wave, jumped up–
but couldn't catch up to the board (the Pacific's so quick).
I tried another one, shoulder high, breaking right, I dropped into
the rush and flow. And then – I took another one – head high –
right at the peak, made the drop, hunkered down, and sped along

a moving wall of spirit blue peeling above my eyes.
memorable. sweet. Gracias, Senor Jesus.

session dos, domingo tardes
High tide returned, a lover seeking its mate but never its match.
Stoked and primed for another wet encounter with majesty
I couldn't wait to take my board and mount those waves.
I paddled with all my strength past each foaming white break to where
the water shimmers, to where surfers wait for consummate sets
shaped heady from a southwest swell. And I was ready to go.
I lined up a shoulder, set the angle, made the drop into a plunging
right that quickly closed and I pulled out. I did the same again.
But on the third, the wall held up in offshore winds and I hung in—
pure bliss, a kiss of ocean's breath. I peeled before the peel,
drinking the thrill until I crashed in the crush of the froth.
Paddling back out I braved three more heady waves, each time pearling
in the steepness of the drop, throwing me headfirst in plunging wash.
Remo, remo, remo – paddle, paddle, paddle – back to the break
where I finally caught another wave. Gracias, Senor Jesus.

session tres, Lunes manana
Graced with a second day of sweet strong surf, two feet overhead,
offshore wind, a little bigger than yesterday, just as clean and potent.
I entered the warm surf before the eastern cruising sun crested
the Nicoya junglemountains. I had the beach to myself and God,
as I watched each wave mount to a head with shoulders breaking
both to the right and left. I paddled parallel to the deepest break
looking for a shoulder and took a nicely pitched left, riding the wall
with some movement on a mounting peeling surging crest.
After some more paddling and some short rides, I charged
a right break, made the drop, and for first time at Nosara
got a little movement up and down the moving face.
Before the session was done I got another sweet ride and felt so good,
so allright, for an old guy catching a few waves and some light.

session quatro, Lunes tardes
Everyone who surfs Guyones knows the one palm on the playa.
That's where the waves pitch and heave, that's where the waves
either grace you or crush you – the best go there, not me, the pitch
too steep for my stiff knees. I had been walking with my wife
and, oh well, that's where I ended up going, straight out from the palm,
the place my sons would go. My spirit wasn't right, nor my body
to take the peeling spill, but I made two of them–the thrust, the drop,
the push, the flop in white wash (quick rush but too quick to grasp).
I prefer a longer glide over higher plunge. Tired, I bellied in.

session cinco, Martes manana
The third day. Symbolic I'd say. Two years ago it was breakthrough.
So this, the third day, I feel rejuvenistic. I'm as up as the waves–
headhigh sets and building, a thrilling peel I could feel even before
I hit the waves. Two rights to kick things off, then a decent backside,
smooth and controlled. (I'm in the groove–Pura vida! Tuanis ma'e!
Gracia Senor Jesus.) I paddle back out (remo, remo, remo)
confident I could catch another right *if* I have the guts to charge.
Seeing it build, I took it at the apex, dropped in, took the plunge
on my knees, then quickly found my feet just in time to take
a long peeling wave, a pure curl of natural glory
reeling just overhead, face to face with epiphanic wonder,
so quick so potent so over in a moment, in a flash, like a life –
some say it doesn't last but it does, you know it – it's spirit.
Gracias Senor Jesus.

session seis, Martes tardes
I was as pumped for the next session as were the waves
which had brought gifts of grace to an old soul surfing.
At first, I took a steep right, made it out ahead of powerful
surf surging behind me, then paddled back out – O Lord! –
with moaning shoulders, then sped off on the edge of a peeling left,
rode it with some movement on my old board down the wave.
Paddled back and waited for another set, hopefully one to the right.

But when a gorgeous left presented itself, I rode it for all its length –
a long, sweet backside break – gracias Senor Jesus.

session siete, Miercoles manana
I had, I confess, been pushing myself beyond my bones.
Each night in the jungle I broke into feverish sweat
as I listened to the wind and waves, to the monos howling,
the dogs barking, the armadillos scurrying in the leaves.
I was sick but would not have it, as I awoke long before dawn
and carried my board down the jungle path, passed the cemetary
to the playa surging with headhigh olas, bonitas y poderosas
with hardly any offshore wind, just a breeze. I started the morning
with a long left (not as long as yesterday) but it was so good.
I paddled back (in the high tide it was not too arduous)
then dropped in on a nice headhigh ride, which I rode to shore
and rested. I paddled back out with great vigor–a beach break
doesn't surrender–and soon caught a super left, long, sweet, good,
followed by two decent rights and another left–I could have gone
all day, but I was weakening and stiffening, as was my will
to push my chilling bones, so I sat and watched the never-tiring sea
and the young men who don't know they'll grow old like me.

That afternoon I did not surf – the tide was too low as was my strength.
My wife and I walked up to the northern crest overlooking Nosara's
craggy cliffs, where we could scan the sea meeting land –
the sea pacific, serene, uncruel, moving yolk slow,
spreading into all the rocky corners of playa Guiones –
but then as some zombie quickened from the dead, it rises,
builds, breaks, spills, a wash of ghosts peeling into and out of sight.
Crazed surfers, looking much like lonely planks awash,
ride these zephyrs and know it's cool to have caught some glory
before it graves. Yet what amazes more is that the ocean cannot
like some leviathan unleashed swallow beach, mountain, earth, man
because some commanding voice stills its swell and lunge.

session ocho, Juves manana
As I got weaker, so did the surf; it dropped a foot or two
to head high sets, but still was glassy, gorgeous, inviting
and I in my weakness couldn't resist. I gathered my will,
waxed my board, strapped my leash, and fixed my sight
on catching some rides. And I, by grace, caught a streaming
left off the shoulder, three good rights in a row – one so sweet
I couldn't help but holler, though there was no one who could hear
over the pounding pulse of the rhythmic push and pull.
Exhilirated yet overly exhausted, I paddled against my mind
to catch just one more (you know) and took a wave to shore –
gracias Senor Jesus.

session nueves, Viernes manana
The morning brings a northwest swell, with sets two feet overhead.
poderosa. bonita. poderosa oleajas. potent pounding peeling.
I have to talk my body into going out. My shoulders rebel as I move
my board painfully forward. The young men make it easy.
They paddle through all five lines of broken surf, duckdiving,
bobbing, buoyant, they seem to float to the deepest break
more than a hundred yards out, while I–this old man of a body–
am ducking, bailing, gathering my board by the leash, paddling
five yards deeper, being pushed back four by another breaking surge.
"Senor Jesus, auxille me!" with added exertion, grunts, groans, and grit
I make it to the offing (I think) and then an eight–foot wave rises Leviathan,
uncaring my fate, to crush me in its wake. And I go tumbling.
Still I persist, not willing to be conquered. I bail. duck. gasp. groan.
Another falls on my head. another. another. I am exhausted
beyond breath. But I persist like some crazed soul not willing
to be old. I make it to the deepest cleanest break. Laying stiff
on my board, breath gone, heart pounding, I encourage my body
to be right and study the oncoming sets, to see which glacis
I can take. "Here it comes, man. Want it." But I'm too deep
to take the drop. I pull out before I take the thrust. Minutes pass.
I rest, gather my soul like a fisherman reeling in a monstrous fish.

I know I have to make it or get caught in the crash, wash,
jungle of froth. "Here it comes. Want it, man," I say to myself.
"This one's for you." I paddle, align my board to take the right.
I'm out ahead to take the thrust, the drop down glacis to the bottom
of the face – and hold like the wind coming off the mountains
in the ride, slide, glide, rush – I can't believe I'm face to face
with this unveiling of creation, this instant revelation, this spirit wave.
I take its epiphanic strength into myself, its power as my own.
I cannot say the wave and I are one – that's for Spirit God,
but I have joined a moment of God afresh God creating.
That is worth celebrating. Gracias Senor Jesus.

Sabado manana
The evening before and into the morning we heard strong winds
rolling off the mountains, washing trees and air into fresca verde
and raro azure. I woke at dawn and walked the gnarly jungle path
to the sea, passing a Tico who greeted me with "Pura vida."
"Si. Pura vida," I replied. The waves were strong and long
but breaking far too quickly down the line for anyone like me
to catch a wave. The offshore gusts were far too bold and brave.
Not even the young made it out that morning. The ocean was alone.

December 7-14, 2002
Playa Guiones, Nosara, Costa Rica

Note: since this was journalistic writing, I did not accent the Spanish
words.

62

40. couldn't make it out

the bombs are falling in Baghdad.
our plane to Hawaii shut down.
terrorists are rousing their religion.
the Atlantic is storming furiously.

I couldn't make it out

I tried to push against the crazy waves.
even the young men were defeated.
the wind wins. always the wind.
whether it's over the ocean or sands.

they couldn't make it out

the bombs keep falling in Baghdad.
bodies fall over. empires fall over.
whether evil or good. the wind wins.
always the wind over the ocean and sands.

no, I couldn't make it out

slim dictators rise and fall. governments
push hard and pall. the waves mount, plunge,
storm the sands. the water is winning.
the wind is strong. stronger than any man.

no, I haven't made it out

the waves wash over the sands.
the winds wash over their bodies.
always the winds. always the waters.
and those who try to make it out.

March 20, 2003

41. earthrise sun

I caught the earthrise sun this morning
     in a slit between two sheaths of clouds
one hanging on the water like a lover
     the other hanging from the sky like a thief.
As the sun passed through these, it lingered
     just long enough in between to mean something.
I snatched this sign and ran it to the sea
     where I surfed the day by waves by storm,
as ghosts of water fell on breaks and peaks
     turning them velvet, soft, supple, sheen.
While thunder hollered on the hazed horizon,
     I slid down smooth silver cresting peaks
and joined our creator, as rain from heaven
     dropped oceans and surfers mounted seas.

April 25, 2003
surfing at Pawleys Island

42. perfect day

sunny skies. offshore wind. storm kicking waves
        a hundred miles out. blessed surf – sublimely shaped

breaking right and left in a serene northwest.
        at first I have them to myself. then others come,

mostly friends. so I don't mind sharing surge,
        slide, glide, splurge. the wave jumping high, tubing,

peeling down the line, as I ride long lefts from peir
        to the groin. and rights all the wave back again.

others do the same as I paddle back out. some hoot.
        some holler. mostly the ocean sings. it soothes,

it moves, as spirit sustains. wind and sea and sun
        and man in confluence: evidence that God is good.

May 2, 2003
Pawleys Island Pier

43. surfer and dolphin

Not much surf today, to speak of, rather slim –
     small knee-high waves pushed by southern winds.
I was about to go home when there appeared
     a pod of sleek dolphins, an epiphany of the sea
pushing out its best creatures like flowers into sun.
     I paddled out among them, an alien to eternal swimming,
drawn to these aqua angels who glide the sea like wind,
     who spirit the depths yet breathe like me oxygen.
As I lay on my board I pray they find me friend,
     not shark, not darkness, not shade, for I cannot tandom
with them. But there is a moment we share in our rare air
     before they slide back to sea and I stroke back to beach:
for a few flashed seconds we meet above the waters,
     even face to face–a sleek gray bottlenose with grin and I
open-mouthed taking it all in, as he headed a jellyball
     again and again ahead of him–sea soccer just for fun!

July 10, 2003
Atlantic Ocean off Pawleys Island

66

44. surfing with my sons

I have surfed with them after squalled suncast,
in a flush of torrent treading the beach,
bending palms, winging from the northeast,
where wetness completely wraps the earth–
yes, we have surfed a riot of waves.

I have surfed with them when the sky is peace
and sun is brisk until it slowly crawls to dusk,
when the waves are clean and breaking open
like cotton scattered in the wind, chasing us
down the face of bliss and laughter.

I have surfed with them the tonic sea in tall winds,
sliding down glacis, gliding smooth and serene.
I never want it to stop, and they don't tire of being with dad
as my shouts mingle with the roar: "Nice ride!" "Cool turn!"
And we paddle back out for more.

Summer 2003
for John and Peter

45. catching waves together

Though it used to be, I'm told, one of the few
      East Coast competition spots, Pawleys Island
isn't world class surf. But some days it's epic.
      And many days good enough for we locals
who know what to look for and when–
      by tide, pier, groin, by wind, storm, moon.
We'll get pounding nor'easters winter into spring
      and we'll have them all glorious to ourselves
till summer surf comes with green vacationers
      and lots of new faces taking occassional breaks
pumped by thunderstorms and southwest winds.
      All of them exodus before autumn springs for us
again with tropical swells and hurricane surges–
      the swollen ocean all pregnant with waves!
It's festal to paddle out in September with friends,
      some to the north, and others to the south of the pier.
The goofy-footers taking peeling lefts, the longboarders
      waiting outside to catch stretched lines,
the shortboarders ripping, cutting, spinning, spraying–
      while I prefer to slide, ride, and glide.
No matter. All of us glow and brim with the hollering sea
      and wear ourselves out like flattened beach.
That night when I close my eyes for sleep, I see swell after
swell
      rise, form, peel, churn, surge, crash, mush, foam.
And I catch faces of waves and friends in the surging sea,
      epiphanies of creator Christ flowing free and fresh.

September 2003

46. before earth arises

solid black, the sheet wrapped across God's face
    slowly splits, as sea separates from sky,
as light rips away darkness, unpeeling it, diminishing it
    to what it isn't, transforming all the hung clouds
to brilliant coral as the band broadens, illumines,
    plumes, penetrates the sky with flare more salmon
than heaven–as all comes alive with light–
    my face. my spirit. the azure lure behind mauve clouds.
the gulls circling, cawing, clutching the seabreeze
    the dolphins purling a lighter sea, sucking lighter air–
and all this before earth arises and I paddle out to waves!

47. dolphin dawn

Emerged from the silver sea
     a hump of bestial beauty
levitating a moment between
     aquatic and aerotic worlds
then with brimming face puggy and serene
     pushed a glow into everywhere dark—
before taking a quick breath of light
     and plunging into invisible silver.

Though the rest of the day was gray
     I breathed lighter
thinking how close I got to God.

48. I return like morning to the sea

The summer air is crisp on Pawleys Island
      from an offshore wind holding up waves
giving them sleek faces with hoary heads
      on the swollen Atlantic, rolling, unscrolling
in apocalyptic blue at sunbreak in birthed light.
      As beachcombers rise I ride some peeling
breaks, while my golden retriever gazes, waits,
      then wanders off in search of minnows
sallied into shallows, sucked back in undertow.

      As I paddled out I admire pelicans wing horizontal
to the sea, surfing the air just before the peeling waves:
      one turns toward the sun, rises on wing span,
dives with tucked pinions into a swirling school,
      emerges with a mullet in its gullet, lifts its throat
to the heavens, and swallows the wriggling bread.

      As I lay on my board scanning the billows
rising up and rolling, a pod of grey dolphins butterflies
      across the vista opposite the pelicans.
They circle, leap, flap fins and dive, as they call their own
      to join the net around a heap of swelling blues.

Further out I am startled by a stingray as big as day
      rocketing the water with angelwings and devilhorns
sprouting from its head and skin as smooth
      as dolphin, gray as shark, terrifying as imagination.

In all of this the sun is silent, pelicans are silent,
      dolphins are silent, and so are the blues and ray.
I am silent, my dog is silent, and so is the horizon.
      Only the breaking waves break the silence.

71

The silent God has watched night, watched stars,
        heard the sun rise and break open day like bread.
And that is why I return like morning to the sea,
        whether the waves are not or good.

July 15, 2004
Pawleys Island, South Carolina

49. somewhere between dream and seem

I trudged out of the sea thinking I had just surfed waves
I had dreamed and not the waves that just had been.
I can tell you about them—they were headhigh, gnarly,
driven by straight eastern wind as before a hurricane
but when I came out of the water after the last wave.

I didn't know if I had stepped out of water or dream—
one of those from my menagerie of wierd waves
I've ridden in backyards, highways, viaducts, tunnels,
creeks, inland and out, in winter and in heat.

Perhaps I'm just as much dream as the reality
of what I've done and am—two beings both each other,
a seen and seer, facing each other strangely familiar.

50. Spirit souls the sea

Earth rises to meet this morning's glow,
Spirit souls the sea, breathes into waves, wind climbs,
    billows, heaves brute bends, buckle, gnarl, cave,
while beachcombers trim, brim, bend, curl, hurl
    in the wave of, crest of, flung fetch of welter,
whether borreal, austral, euroclydion, or western—
    the four winds of zoatic pneuma verve, gush
zephyrs, sprout bulbous, spill unctuous, cleave
    reefs, island man, smashing cliffs, rock
and those who mean to surf the meanest break.
    Most have to take the gentler smoother roll,
the sweeter stuff of waves, the lighter
    and smaller peels, not breaking them to coral—
while you, my son, brave the rising leviathans
    with rip, spin, cut, swirl, spray, and smile.

for Peter on his 22nd birthday, April 26, 2004
Wilderness, northwest coast, Puerto Rico

51. hummingbird in hurricane

We hurry inland from falling floods
swollen seas birthing outrageous rush
    in fast force of wind mounting waves
climbing up the back side and tumbling
over the front in a spill of white upon white
    in seasurge crush and push of dunes and air
      erasing the horizon smearing the line
between firm terrain and watery main.

A mile inland there's no sun than what's believed—
    as the slim trees bend shiver break
weeping willows uproot drooping
    elms unbranch and fly like pelicans
pines curve contort twist and vault
as we hear leaf-sizzle treesnap crash
    and the hurricane raining down wind.

During this assault I was startled to spot
    the hummingbird who lives in our woods
gripping a flailing untresilled magnolia branch
flapping in gusts like a lose haulyard—
and with wings whirling cyclone fast and furious
    helicopting in the horrific hurricane attack
    long enough to sip some nectar from a cup
and then speed like wind through bending pines.

August 14, 2004
Hurricane Charlie

52. the boy who tried to cross

the sun pulled the windy sky into a dive
        of maroon splattering the horizon
the full moon followed like a victor's horse
        dragging a host of vanquished stars
towing a swollen sea into the southern inlet
        dumping whitecapped billows
into a turgid creek ripping round our island

as the tide surged and undertow sucked
        where ocean and inlet mingle
the water jumped turned twisted and growled
        old leviathan resuscitated

there we stood next to this awesome denizen
        a few feet from certain drowning
while sirens wailed louder than the roar
        fingers started pointing and eyes strained
a crowd began to gather muttering ultimate questions
        no one could hear above the booming surf
as rescuers strapped in orange lifevests
        sped into the inlet one craft after another
looking deep for the boy who tried to cross

South Inlet, Pawleys Island

53. what the sea sees

Absorbing sunbreak and moonfall longer than bones,
       earth's eyeball, half the globe filming
looks upward, not at us, peering at galaxies of God,
       while this turf has sucked the best and mean
and is the heavier for having taken down.

Not the ocean that survives with soul,
      it has a way of breathing.
Nothing I can say could make it swell—
       dwarfed by its majesty I am dumb
but not deaf—the seawinds are my prophets.

Empires peak and crash—Babylon, Greece, Rome,
England, and other proud predicted powers—
      but the sea sees none of them,
nor does the seawinged seahawk hovering wind,
      scanning waves, eyes fixed on ocean
until catching a phosphorescent flash of bluefish
      falls quick as light with open talons.

They will be this again and again
      the sea the sun the hawk the wind
long after all of us have fallen into humus
      and this land we've called United States.

54. Hurricane Katrina

Unmothered brute beast bends nature
        bullies seas into heave, growl, ghoul
not descriminating whose marrow it sucks—
shores, homes, trees, and thinner structures, man—
as it dumps heaps of water deeper than despair
        that there's no God of Noah near.

While smothered souls give up their ghosts
        to spirited places where Spirit roams,
others climb to attics and axe their way to air
and hovering angels rapturing their fear.
They are not, as desired, winged to refuge
        but to where nothing is doing human well.

Here and there among the groping diaspora,
        saints appear as living light unearthing cheer,
beaming hope, absorbing pools of tears.
And this is what makes me think there's still
some deity left from the God who humaned us
and that his Spirit can inspire us to grasp
        that grace is given when faith is not.

August 2005

55. september surf

As I stiff a sandy trail from marsh to ocean
      I hear what the waves appear to be
and can't wait to immerse my head in water
      warmer than the air. I'll push my legs to bend
one more session as I come to where sea lands
      and moves a man still strong enough to paddle
and aged enough to know I won't always
      have strength to break beyond the breaking surge.

But for this day I am good enough, as I am drawn
      by the cresting and curling sea exploding
into whiteness from dark nothing. I'm awed by swells
      mounting to shore with epiphanic faces.
It's amazing that the rude ocean lines up in the end:
      beachcomber after beachcomber rakes
shoals, beach, and brim in even strokes.

And all this because a hurricane churns the Atlantic our way,
      pushing northeastern waves for days on days—
in sweet swells pearling to the surfer's left
      blowing spindrifts in occasional offshore gusts,
or in strong rushes shoaling too swiftly to catch.

The day before the hurricane hits, I surf to the end
      of my strength, until the last glory of dusk,
as the clouds overhead clutch as much sheen as they can
      in an eerie glimmer brightening before it dims.

In the morning the outer bands circle our way,
      dropping sky into sea, pummeling ocean into sand;

by afternoon the typhoon has swallowed sun
       and risen leviathan in ocean lunging at land,
pounding the pier, crushing a few crazed surfers—

       it's wild, it's wierd, it's the wind conquering earth
whenever it can. And it does it best with heaps of water
       so beastly beautiful, so awfully powerful,
so close to killing and kind to quicken water into waves.

September 4-14, 2005,
when hurricane Ophelia was spinning off
the South Carolina coast for days on end

56. windRider

While dolphins glide glacis with the grace
      of those who've lived ocean long as sea
and pelicans scoot down pearlingBreaks
      with wings extended into cherubim
            I push my body into morningWake
      and ride the sea that rides the wind
all the while praying that none of this will end—
      the wildWind surging horizons,
            the bold sun pushing blue into the sky
            the September air whipping through my hair—
as I steer my board and paddle the crests.

      "You spirit the wave like a pelican whose wings
never touch water, o wind and windRider—
            you are sun that stirs weather, waveMaker,
      you are the brave who breaks waves and takes waves
fierce and fat," as I lay flat, so much smaller than water,
      so much thinner than the tall wind,
            and wait for yet another swell.

When the sea leaps, my spirit leaps, your shape leaps into my feet
      as we catch the translucent swell and flash down the line
glassing before us, transparent as God, smooth as light,
      and breaks behind us into a million ghosts leaping into white
as quickly as they die—while I in that quickened rush
      of wind catching sea and water chasing water
feel the windRider surfing the wave with me.

57. the voice

when a groundswell rolls in, bellowing,
billowing, curling, trimming, feathering
percussing arpeggio across this archipelago
the sea becomes my kithara and muse.
I immerse myself to fetch that voice
I first heard between cadence and crash—
the voice that spills from lips of waves
in the timbre of variegated aeolian peaks
cresting to crescendo falling in moreno;
somewhere in there between the breaks
I hear the oracle that makes life sense
seagull caw, seahawk silent glide, pelican dive
into an ocean more majestic than awe.
rise. wind. wave. spirit. verve. I call
God who is coming God who has come,
the end is nothing more than what has been:
wind singing sea, sea surging bends and breaks—
in long strong stress waves musicate
the voice
in long strong stress waves musicate—
wind singing sea, sea surging bends and breaks,
the end is nothing more than what has been:
God who is coming, God who has come.
rise. wind. wave. spirit. verve. I call
into an ocean more majestic than awe,
seagull call, seahawk silent glide, pelican dive;
I hear the oracle that makes life sense
somewhere in there between the breaks
cresting to crescendo falling in moreno
in the timbre of variegated Aeolian peaks,
the voice that spills from lips of waves
I first heard between cadence and crash.
I immerse myself to fetch that voice
percussing arpeggio across this archipelago
billowing, curling, trimming, feathering
when a groundswell rolls in bellowing.

58. He moves

He moves between the breaking seas
    in dark mystery.

Pelicans wing along the peeling waves.

The eyes of God, the face of man—
    you are not quite one of us.

The disk drops darkness and it is cold.

He makes eternity palpable, almost
    attainable. Almost.

The clouds eat sunsets and are gone.

He lingers somewhere near the broken
    soul and quiet breath.

Seagulls and pelicans warm winter waters.

Some say he appears as dolphin. As savior
    of the drowning.

Dogs chase waves. Men chase dogs and days.

Too fast. Too swift the kick from here to there.
    But he makes it.

I am not warm enough for winter.

59. slow beauty, slow circle

Mirroring mackerel skies, flocculate clouds, sun so bright
it shouts, a cirrus seacreek annulates Pawleys Island,
    a corolla round a cay that's been hurricaned
to death and resurrects. Each sunrise is breath.
The oscillating tide pushes the creek high, pulls it low
    in pulmonary flow, sucking sea air into its throat,
    exhaling a scent so pungent it's poignant.
I sit creekside hearing breaking waves off to my east,
waves that have beached spermwhales, buried billions
    of unsouled shells, broken bodies into sand,
and hurled at man more mysteries than explanations.
    On a sunworn dock reaching into this savannah,
I admire a swallowtail hanging summersun on amaranth
its wings shutting, papyrus pressed, and flinging open
an aperture into ever slowness. A bullfrog not about
to move the day bellows in sawgrass not hurrying sun
or shade, as yonder I eye a gator gliding as quiet as time,
his stare never aging, his eyes not fearing that I am.
    I spot a goldeyed snowy egret ghosting forward
with slow step in silent shallows bending its S-curved
neck in half a circle; the other penciled by imagination.
It's all a slow circle drawn diurnal,
a continual annulating in euphotic waters where
acropetal auroles appear everywhere from nowhere.
I didn't throw a stone or cast a line or dip my toe.
And there were no raindrops I could feel.
My thoughts drift into shades of brown smeared across
the marsh lit by summersun burning out the cusp of day.
    Does anything here that imagines anything else?
I wish I had no other mind as I sit here watching
lightfall spring native night, moonshadows crawl around,
and stars birthed in some novae billion lightyears past
just now being grasped.

60. Christmas tsunami (2004)

the ocean was drawing back into itself
like a god pulling in a deep breath

children frolicked on the revealed seafloor
jumping in small waterholes of the new foreshore
while their parents explored the uncovered terrain
a few locals came down to fetch some gasping fish
while others stood back warily

    having never seen the ocean rush backwards

perhaps it was the new moon's tug and pull

out to sea some scuba divers descended
        into their dive and were rocked
    by a strangely strong underwater roll
yet they ascended into calm and sun

a couple sunning on their sailboat deck
spotted one ripple like a long pipe speed by them
and pass underneath
    they studied it as it humped toward land
mounting ever bigger into a bloated seaserpent

    some Tai fishermen even deeper in the deep
felt a wave pass underneath them and rock their ship

a surfer sat on his board scanning the horizon
    searching for some oncoming swell

he saw was flat sky flat sea and the line where they meet
until out of nowhere the sealine gobbled the sky—
        he dropped to his stomach and paddled for his life

in Yala Sri Lanka and the coasts of the Indian ocean
elephants chained to palms snapped their chords
        and lugged children to higher ground
water buffalo, langur monkeys, leopards sensing terror
                broke to the mountains
as did the Jarawa, Onge, Sentilese, and Andamanese
        the natives who've gathered nature long

but not the tourists and some locals
        who continued to comb uncovered beaches
heads down looking around for shells and such—
not seeing the oncoming rush but hearing a drone
        growling like jet engine thrust
looked up and out to sea

                as the horizon transmogrified
                into a dark blue leviathan mounting
                a black smoked seamonster
                with frothy head and mammoth face
                with rush faster than thought, higher than God
                a wave that did not curl or break after it built
                but pushed heaps of apollyon with watery fists

grabbing their children by their hands they ran
        as the torrent ate land beneath their feet
ripping babies from mother's grip, hurling bodies
into palms, suffocating children in foam,
chasing the swiftest sprinters into jungles,
sucking the strongest swimmers
        past floating corpses ripped back to sea

85

and this was just the first almighty crash
on that sunny sunday morning after Christmas

the second swelled like hoods of a giant cobra in the sky
charged more hellion than apollyon rushing shores
like Herod's dark army on Bethlehem's streets
     stripping mothers of their children
     in death worse than rape
     spewing seawater everywhere people can't drink
     spewing corpses everywhere people can't fathom
the living swim through them, those clinging to palms
or hanging to balconies watch them pass—their lovers,
their mothers, their sons and daughters beyond
their grasp as the quick seasurge sucks as swiftly back

some swallow water because they have no power
others swallow sea to hasten death

half the people in half the debris fall to the earth
of broken bodies mangled cars, hotels, and boats
the other half are raked back to sea like seaweed
returned the next few mornings as bloated oblations
to some god gone crazy or god gone dead

*

The man on the Sri Lanka beach stood there caught
between lifeand death and didn't know which as he saw
the seabeast mounting He heard it growling
When it pounced on him he was tumbled into watery
darkness into layers of deep waters unlit abysmal
obsidian waters swimming in pelagic depths
going deeper and darker This blackness was so dark
there were no shadows no gradation from black to grey

Obsequious this darkness wrapped around itself took
itself over demonized itself as darkness possessed
with itself It was very slow blackness the kind of blackness
that's going nowhere because there was nowhere to go
but deeper darkness There was no peeling away
no stripping down to something other than darkness
which fell heavy as chaos There used to be something other
than watery darkness but for now earth was drowning
and all that was in it He was tumbling in the darkness
of azoatic obsidian There was nothing called sky horizon
space or breath Earth trembled under the pressure
The subterranean shook and cracked the sea making waves
breaking into other waves across sealong fetches waves
mounting in the offing rising leviathan crashing mushing
reforming mounting cresting collapsing intermingling
with a million other waves colliding swirling going nowhere
in oceans of confusion in lull and lunge lunge and lull
water falling upon water with no shores to take
the fall Liquid cymbal clangs with liquid cymbal in dark
sound of it all Rush and roll Roll and rush on shoals
sandbars reefs Deep from caverns the waves leaped lunged
plunged spilled fell from dark pitch crash crush roar sizzle
The surge the slosh the rush crush crash between each
fetch and flush in long stretches of nothing but darkness
pushing darkness into blacker spaces Faceless mirrorless
unconscious water making itself seas drowning itself
in listlessness and yaw in plunge to deep in depths of gone
going deeper A strangle of water suffocating earth
A liquid ring as round as nimbus moon but no glow
only gloom in the dirge of surge upon surge flapping
fishless fetches of lonely stretches of horizonless seas
seizing seas A tumble of black rolling into black and back
again into nothing but wash wave lunge surge lull crash
flush churn This sea a monster heaving reeling in heavy

wetness in dark so fat nothing could wriggle
between the cracks lies leviathan behemoth on paws
fanning its serpentine tail over what used to be fecund
lumined soil All is Waterwithoutlight Deepwithoutlife
A desert of sea everywhereGoingnowhere
for there was no horizon no separation of sea from sight
no beach no wind of light to open to break bleak bands
and hardly a survivor left.

A few crawled through the nightsea to see some spirit
smack damp black in half and an eyelid crack the dawn
The sultry shroud lifted and the single eye unveiled pealed
sky beamed seas The lit disk emberorange surged hot from
burning styx exorcised murkiness swallowed shadows
between waves made cool waters rise and ghost from earth
It was a day for wind taking light and throwing it all
around between the shades and troughs for drawing
the long thin horizon line as circular as an eye
It was a day for epiphanies of color for the parousia
of the sun's soft skull rupturing the oval horizon flushing
it bloodshed red raw and strange more crimson than color
for slaying black leviathan of its lair and lore.

But on some of the islands there was not a soul to scan
the ocean sun in hue shift more subtle than skyshift
afterstormblack bottomblack sharkblack with yellowfoam
turning brown greenbrown in swarms of waves one after
another breaking in bluefroth into so many greens
hundreds of them more than the forest trees and plants
a roving jungle of verdant greens holding sunrays lit greens
in translucent beams springgreens summercool bluegreens
layered greens in euphotic shadows There was not a soul
to catch the colorswitch from murkiness to virescence
the mellowing of duskgreen from emerald to reseda
and all the in-betweens of hazel jade aquamarine.

88

*

Satan walked the shore and counted the dead
mostly children and women who couldn't outrun the flood

Jesus walked the sea and counted those who saved
Themselves and those who just were saved:

the man who jumped from a wrecked train
        cluttered with floating corpses
                and found refuse on a nearby rooftop

the boy who gripped the luggage rack
until the water subsisded

        the family
        who grabbed
        their hotel towels
        climbed palms
        and tied
        themselves on
        till dusk

                a fisherman who
                climbed a pole
                with daughter
                on his back
                and two sons
                in each arm
                holding and holding
                slipping and slipping
                until the two fell
                into the surge
                and seemed to drown

later they were found half buried under sludge
and handed to him who cried and sighed,
"why did God choose to save my children
when he chose to let so many others die?"

an Indian boy clinging to a treetop
who heard his mother scream
his name,"Ardiyansah!"
before she succumbed to sea

another boy, Chia-ni, flung onto a coconut tree
who wailed a day and night before he was taken down

a young Tai washed downstream
who saved himself by clutching riverbank roots
as the water kept surging overhead—
he struggled to surface several times
only to hear his mother scream,
"where are you? where are you, my son?"

another Tai boy who believed he breathed underwater
until he was flung to safety on the shore of a jungle

a Hong Kong couple clinging to a mattress
careening through the streaming living and dead

a new baby sleeping on a floating mattress

a six year old, Zoe Shiu, grasping a cushion

a Swedish toddler tossed into sludge
rescued by Americans and restored
to his father's heart bereaved of love

the 26 orphans
whose thin peninsula
was being engulfed
by water cascading over the lagoon on one side
and pouring in from the estuary's mouth on the other
whose Christian leader, Daylan Sanders
quickened by Scripture
(when the enemy comes in like a flood,
the Lord's Spirit raises up a standard)
gathered them quickly into a boat
that he steered straight into the oncoming tsunami
                    knowing their only hope
            was not to outrun the surge
but to get on top and ride it out like Noah's ark

        the children on a Thai shore
        who were hoisted to the back of an elephant
        that had been brought to the beach to entertain

the son of Sangreta, an Indian mother
who with three young sons and only two hands
shouted to her oldest, "Run, run, Dinakartan!"
but he fled into their hut where he was sure to drown
had not it been for their old yellow dog, Selvakumar
who urged him to the jungle and his mother's arms

        the man trapped three days and nights
        under the wreckage of his boat and house

the man buried under debris for two long weeks
        who lived on nothing but faith

Satan scoured the sea and counted the floating corpses
Jesus walked the waters and saw the few who rode it out

the Indonesian man, Rizal, who was found afloat
    after three days of clinging to an uprooted tree

an Indonesian woman, Malawati, who was pulled from sea
    after five days of riding a sago palm
whose bark and fruit she ate, as fish and sun did the same

a Sri Lankan fisherman, Mohammed Sarfudeen,
who clung to his capsized boat for three days and nights

the fishermen who survived eight fiercesome days
    under ruthless sun on a drinkless sea

*

in the days after, if you could call them days,
    mothers groped the shore
for bodies to appear
        fathers wandered the debris
wondering if it's better to be the stench
    or smell

    others searched desperate
photos of the living and lists of the deceased
    trying to match the two

uncertainty is excruciating
    but is it greater than the agony of a mother
falling headlong when she discovers her child
    drowned under a mound of sludge?
or the anguish of those whose children
    slipped from their watery fingers?

92

all along the Sri Lankan coast
bodies were scattered like broken shells
        emptied of their souls

Hindus burned corpses quickly hoping to kill memory
        hoping fire is stronger than water
                and water is not longer than love

a monk found a corner in an overcrowded Buddhist temple
        to meditate and chant, but he couldn't transcend
his painful thoughts, "Siddartha has no answer for death,
only for suffering—yet not this. The sea is not illusion."

a priest in a makeshift morgue
struggling once again to find some words for the dead
        and words for the living,
thought but did not say, "there's no theodicy here—
though some have seen miracles, God seems to hide
        behind faces blurred and wrenched with agony,
from eyes raised to heaven,
from that bereft mother hunched there mumbling blame
and that father rummaging for his child
among a pile of bodies about to be bulldozed down a pit.
The earth, for all its sweetness and wonder,
is a dangerous place to live and a good place to leave."

a Sunni imam in an Indonesian mosque on friday morning
knowing he's supposed to tell the congregation
        that punishment falls on those who do not follow
Allah's laws and have been seduced by Western thought,
forced himself to castigate those who lost their children
        and those who lost their faith—
citing the Qur'an, he proclaims with trembling face,
        "accept your fate, for this is Allah's will."

around the globe theologians debate:
     some saying this is the way it's always been—
there's no theology here just tectonics
       and humans in nature's path;
others surmising it's all because of the fall,
whatever that's supposed to mean;
     others declaring God has the power
     to save and destroy
      to give life or not
     if that is his will and way;
and still others imagining it could be
     God is taking us away to a better place—
not in one apocalyptic gulp but in measured scoops

tell that to the stunned stumbling under torrid sun
who have nowhere to find the lights that left them

*

the sea was calm before the throne
     where millions were gathered—
archangels, angels, the living creatures,
     souls and souls and souls and souls—
welcoming the children carried to their shores
     on broken boats, seasoaked debris, and junks.

Children heard the song of those annulating the throne:

"Blessed is the only God,
     the Lord of wind and sea,
the only One having immortality
     and breathing it as living love and life.

You are the only One inhabiting light as Light,
        light no has really seen or could ever know,
the One who creates darkness and brilliance,
        who can inhabit either as sun or shade,
the One who gives life, breath, and being,
        who alone shrouds the secrets of meaning
too deep, too dreadful, too awesome, too high
        for any to comprehend on this side of Light.
You are brute Beauty and awful Glory,
        the Bright behind every gloom,
the shade and sun; you shadow and illumine."

*

the man was spewed out from tumbling darkness
and slammed on shore like a shell breaking its soul
He found himself naked before the Spirit Lord
who asked: does the sea have boundaries I haven't set?
can you tell the surging waves to stop?
have you entered into the ocean's fountains?
have you climbed deep sea mountains?
have you been to the gates of Hades
and peered down the throat of the abyss?
can you say where light is born?
can you tell me where darkness dawns?
can you dawn one morning and douse the sun
at evening in the wet horizon?
can you make each wave rise surge bellow
brim trim peel curl crash froth fizz and disappear?

61. Nosara, another journal

Back to Playa Guiones for the third time
to rare earth and pristine ocean.
I've gotten three years older since—
I worry about my breathing, my strength,
my power against the potent Pacific sea
which on this last day of the year
heaves waves three feet overhead
with leviathan sets swallowing the horizon,
waves I cannot and do not surf.

I watch my son, Peter, slide down these breaks
marveling how his young strength takes
the brute height, fast force, imminent crash
to cut up/ cut back/ whip fast/ fling flash
as in a dance with a beautiful monster.

The first day of the new year brings my handsel:
the waves have dropped to a measure I can handle,
I believe, especially at the north beach
where the waves don't jump so quickly.
My first three rides are shortlived—
almost all whitewater. (Took off too late.)
The fourth, headhigh, is pure liquid blue,
opening up before me a ride down a face
moving quicker than thought and sense—
passing too quickly to retrace its epiphany.
The fifth, nearly as good, rides me into shore
and my mind into Pura Vida.

I am stoked enough to try the afternoon surf
but discover once I'm out there
it's bigger than what I imagined on shore

where I had watched awesome surfers take off down
the wave and whip across the face like wind.
But here I am waiting for some huge kindness
to come my way. When one smaller one rises,
I paddle hard, heart jumping, jump to my feet,
lean back to take the drop, don't wipeout,
and come clean into surging surf rushing me to land.

On the second day of the new year,
I rise earlier than the sun brimming over
the Guanacaste ridges, to see lines of waves
rising, trimming, breaking off to the right
and left, slightly held up in offshore breezes.
I urge my shoulders into paddling
both to get beyond the breaks then into them.
My second ride, shoulder high, is pure wall,
one of the best I've ever been graced with—
gracias Senor Jesus. And so the fourth.
What a thrill to feel a liquid hand moving me,
to see its face appear next to mine, a quick epiphany
of the evanascent Immanent who Is in all,
Through all, and Above all—still there after
the wave disappears into nothing but memory.

On the evening of this sublime day
my wife and I are caught away
into the native vibe of a local band,
the Medicine Show, in which our son,
known here as Papaya Pete, fingers
the guitar and sings a few Spanish songs.
We are swayed by the tropical rhythms
and delighted to hear our son sing so pure.

It's an evening I don't want to stop on the last note,
but we go back under a sky singing with stars
under a moon growing on us each day we're here.

On the third day of the new year
I wake earlier than auroral winds,
amber down the jungle trail,
hear a howler monkey moaning morning,
watch him swing from limb to limb,
as I step over gnarled roots running everywhere,
till I pass the graveyard of a hundred souls
facing the Pacific and Hesperian hopes.

My hope for good waves is answered
by headhigh sets in offshore winds.
I struggle for the first hour, not timing
the cadence of the cant and headwind
which pushes up the tip of my board
no matter how I hard I paddle or inch forward.

After three disappointing rides
frustration rises and my grace wanes.
I calm myself, breathe the Spirit slowly,
and tell myself not to fight the fetch
or battle wind, but take them as God gives.
As I am just okay surfer,
I need things to come together right.
Soon thereafter mercy palaquins my way:
I am carried on a wave whose lips
aperture before me—a flower opening to the sun—
I am pistilled down an aqueous flume.

After a fun morning, I exit the ocean
and walk the beach looking at the stoked
young surfers taking waves with skill, thrill, power.
Sooner than I would like to confess
the ichor will drain from my veins
and exhilaration drop into exhaustion.

My wife and I enjoy the late afternoon
hiking to hotel Nosara set on a promenade
of raw rock standing bold in surging seasplash.
The view from here inspires largeness:
to the south, Playa Guiones, a mile of curved beach
set within peninsulas legging into water;
to the north, Playa Pelada, and beyond that
Playa Nosara, beaches spotted with starved rocks.
I can see the scalloped sea for miles out,
studying the form each wave takes as it nears shore—
how it mounts, peels, pearls, crashes, froths,
and throws whitewater on sea canvas
in fluid shapes, faces, and aqueous forms
only to be followed by another almost like itself
but never the same in the fluid painting of divine design.

On the fourth day of the new year
I come to the beach as early as the sun
and am greeted by chesthigh sets in offshore wind.
Is paradise any better? God's presence is good.
As usual I start slowly—having to get my bones seawet
and sunwarm before they go. After three small rides,
I find the form of many waves and flow!
No cuts. No spins. No spray. Just an adrenergic day
of small S-curves surging down moving walls of liquid glass.

The fifth day resurrects paradise again.
Am I heaven? Chesthigh sets in offshore wind,
waves rising from the bulbous blue sea,
pearling luminous white, inviting beachcombers
trimming left and right, an oldman surfer's delight.
Even still, I must paddle till it aches—
the break forms more than a hundred yards out.

I find the rhythm and roll into several rides
along hyaline swells surging to my right,
one of which is the longest, sweetest yet.
And another surfer lets me take me a left
I'll never forget—both for his coolness
and the ride that keeps flowing in my head.

The sixth day resurrects paradise yet again.
I ask the same question: have I been heavened?
I nearly repeat what I surfed the day before
and I am not at all bored. This must be paradise:
riding the same surf for eternal days—
and I pray there will be eternal waves.

In the evening of the sixth day
black wind roars down the mountain
killing all electricity, breaking palm fronds,
collapsing any newborn waves.

The wind lessens in the morning of the seventh day,
but still is heaving strong, making it hard to drop
into the wave, which crumbles into tumbling froth
as soon as I take off. Nonetheless, a few hold up
and I am pleased to see some aqueous face.

On the morning of the eighth day,
I see what I have come to see so many days
at Playa Guiones: perfect surf in offshore breeze
under a covering of sunlight as twanis as life.
My confidence has risen to another height:
I believe I can take off higher in the crest
and make the drop without a fall.
Four in row—I can't believe it!
And then I paddle to wait the deepest sets.

A beauty is coming. I hesitate for a second,
thinking the Tico down the line will get it,
but I realize he's letting it pass for me.
I paddle hard, looking over my left shoulder
at the wave forming gorgeously. I take it
at its peak and make the drop by leaning back
on my board and then immediately forward
as I'm launched across the face of a gracious wave
that stays held up by the offshore zephyr
for longer than any I remember—
as I glide along eyeing this headhigh hyaline
I realize I'm face to face with miracle in motion,
as close to the quick of creation as I may ever be;
my heart is beating out my mouth
my mind is screaming, "this is my longest ride ever!"—
this wave that is long and sleek, strong and steady,
a beauty of a beast that moves me all the way to shore,
where I dismount my board and sit in awe,
trying to recapture as quick as I could
the sweetest, longest wave I've ever surfed.

As I sit here in bright Costa Rican sunlight
savoring the taste of this wave, realizing
this may never happen in my life again,

101

another surfer walks by, who is nearly as old as I.
When he asks me how I'm doing and I tell,
he nods: "sometimes it all just comes together."

On the ninth day of the new year,
I wake early and move to the sea
with sore legs, aching back, slight headache,
but I am twanis with life. Pura Vida.
A cotamundi crosses my path on the way
to the graveyard leading to the sea.

I read a few names, check their dates,
stretch for awhile soaking in the sun
and sight of swelling chesthigh waves
breaking my way, beckoning my body
to join the cadence of rise, break, glide.

The tenth day is exactly the same:
offshore winds, long lines of chesthigh waves,
which I enjoy all morning long—
slipping down long rights with lots of time
for S-curves and fun, as well as a few lefts thrown in.
I surfed with Bill for awhile, guitarist in Peter's band,
and then went in, exhilirated and exhausted.

On the eleventh day I surfed with Peter, my son,
who catches about four waves to my one.
He never tires of paddling and catching,
twisting, cutting, jumping into air, and landing.
It's so sweet to surf the sea with him,
sharing a common passion for the lving ocean,
enjoying a few exchanges of smiles and rides.
I soak this in, knowing how life passes.

102

On the twelfth day, the last of my visit,
I am so exhausted, I can hardly move.
Nonetheless, I am in Costa Rica
and want to make the best of my vacation.
So I push myself to walk to the seashore,
where I sit under the archway
between sea and cemetery—
behind are rows of silent mounds
crowned with coral crosses facing Hersperian hopes.

Outside past pounding breakers
crowds of surfers sit deep, look west,
bobbing up and down in swelling mounds,
their longboards arching up
like these headstones catching falling sun.
While they wait, passing waves
lilly up, shovel down, and break
into hundreds of hoarheads—
and then they see, as I see, a swell
swallowing the horizon, speeding their way.

A decision quickens into a paddle
with the Almighty— quick drop, heart stop,
crouch at the feet of the immanent Mover
who gives quickened rides on spirited water
down uncertain lines of liquid power
until it froths, hisses, thins, and evanesces.

I rise from the graveyard, walk humbly
into the sea with a surfboard under my arm,
knowing sundown is dropping quickly.

December 31, 2005—January 12, 2006
Playa Guiones, Nosara, Costa Rica

62. seascroll

I catch breath, dive underneath summersaulting break,
surface, bite another wave mount, reel, peel:
out of eternal circular flatness it mounds up
in multiple moving faces, walls up, glistens diaphanous,
bends fistulous, breaks, buckles, falls in percussive rushes.

Looking back I see tumbled sun burst white, turn thin light,
sizzle out, as each wave—quick life—is sucked back to sea.

When ocean reveals itself in flash of opened face,
the cast becomes a voice pitched as apocalypse—
a voice I first heard when the ocean began
hurling revelations so potent I was felled to my knees,
forced to measure my liquesence, the compass of my fetch.

Yet it's so hard to say the mystery I've heard, for as quick
as it's revealed, the sea scrolls itself into a roll I can't read.

Whenever I hear clouds coming and horses running on water,
I paddle into a herd of waves and let one after another pass
until there's one that bends its neck and gallops me to shore.
I know that's why I return again and again like waves—
I have hopes of unraveling lips as I catch a peeling break.

63. sea-spawn

I drink sundawn sea, mouth it moist,
smell lightyears bouncing off the breaks
(supernovae breaking speed)
mingled with fishswim old as God-thought
young as spindrift windkicked—
ah, birdwind, puffs of ocean rinsing morning me

in silent flight eyewise cocked toward surf-face
a string of seabirds streak the peeling line gawking
at sunbroken waves unhiding hundreds of fish in seaspill—
watch: waves, fins, wings all silverbacked whitebellied
dive headfirst in rush thrush of splash, plumage, and gills
quick keel and reappear as bobs in ocean yawn

surfing the moving moment of sea-spawn

64. sea acacia

there were times of singing but it has been way too long
since then—way too deep hide the vowels of joy
for me to well them up again. they were there once
I remember. I recall singing, I remember joy and its taste
but my tongue is saltsoaked, my heart with bad wine,
my bones are shaking, my fingers trip on broken rhyme
my pen moans a broken vessel warped by slanted seawind

in the ancient waters I see long spirits rising and dying
invisible horses churning the waves, angels treading water
onto the broken shore where a sea acacia with sea limbs
crooked by gnarly winds holds terra firma only as long as . . . . .
you've outsung me, old man, but not the sea of winds.
the ocean always wins; it won't paean you or me
as we seagreen and our roots topple upsidedown

105

65. ocean oaks

Ocean old, they sprawl, stretch, gnarl, wear the sea,
      cling trellised to the dropping sky—
their heavy branches having shoved their way
          into sunshine without man or beast
having seen any exertion or manuevering underneath.

As we stroll under them, we're amazed how they tangle
      with heaven, we marvel at the knobby canopy
that shades us, as generations before and beyond,
          and we imagine who layed under their boughs
drooling spanish moss, catching summer breeze
with wind-twisted trunks spiraling skyward
      then downward into bended crook and crawl—
so unlike the erect pines piercing into blue,
          the oaks hang with us—they linger round
our homes and grow on us like longtime friends,
they become our hands with so many clinging fingers
      grasping our longings for everlasting climbs—
this is their sacred glow, that they outlive us
          yet never forsake us like some unearthly soul
seeking release from earth's heavy burdens.

And so we never believe that one could come to an end,
      until our path brings us to a skeleton oak—
its tawny brown ashened, its angels turned to ghosts,
          and its fallen wings dry and brittle
snapping underfoot. Yet still it somehow stands
with no sap sucked from heavy earth; it stands
      heavy among the living. And I don't understand,
no I can't, why its roots wearied of seeking
          and its boughs of stretching—or could it be
that earth tires, letting us all go one by one?

66. thirsty for a drink of spring

northeast gusts whirl off the Outerbanks
pumping line after seismic line of aqua waves
to our south Carolina coast glistening
in the early risen sun
                    winter is done—
May has come: the sea smells so, the sky,
the magnolia blossoms breathing open,
the confederate jasmine climbing into my nose

God knows I've sprung alive into life
as I paddle out past the white breakers
peeling from left to right, as I deep the sea
and see waves rising
                    on the horizon—
Duck diving, clinging to my wood, spitting sea water,
I'm thrilled to catch some super slick rides
down some long lefts. I'm always amazed I ride a wave
and wonder if God gives fins for an old soul to glide

I wish I could do this as long as the sun and sea
but I have only so many Mays to spring me,
more delicious as they pass, like drinking a cold
draught of apple juice
                    after the grass is mown—
the quick coldness plummeting from tongue *
to blood, liberating every thought for a moment,
so that for the time being it just feels so cool
to be a human being, not a human doing

I've been so thirsty for a drink of spring!

107

www.ingramcontent.com/pod-product-compliance
Lightning Source LLC
Chambersburg PA
CBHW060419090426
42734CB00011B/2364